TOWNSHIP

BIZ

FASTRACK

BY TIISETSO MALOMA

Copyright

Contents

4

Foreword by Mongezi Makhalima

There are two myths currently making rounds in the South African economo-sphere:

- While the figures of unemployment in this country are officially estimated at 27%, I have a suspicion that they lie somewhere closer to 40%.
- South Africans are lazy and not entrepreneurial

In order to address the first myth, I propose that South Africa doesn't need more jobs, it needs more entrepreneurs. It is the entrepreneurs that will accelerate the growth of this country. It is entrepreneurs that will dominate the economy of this country. This leads us to the second myth. If you walk through the townships of this country, the corners of the city in this country and you spend time in the DTI offices in Pretoria, you will realise this is far from the truth!

What each of these people need though is mainstreaming! With Skills, knowledge and Support- both financial and non-financial.

But this won't be happen - until entrepreneurs stop waiting for someone to do it. And the government stops waiting to do it. And the FDI's stop waiting. And EDA's stop waiting. If we all started moving in one direction towards this dream, we just might surprise the world.

This booklet is just one person's attempt to shift us there. And I'm with him. Are you?

- - -

Mr Makhalima is currently the MD of Mzantsi Leadership Development, and the director at the Pretoria Centre for Work-Based learning, a professional development outfit that prepares people for entry into the professions of Project Management, Accounting, Coaching & Coaching Psychology, Organisation Development, Local Government and Entrepreneurship.

He is currently the Chairperson and founding member of the Africa Board for Coaching, Consulting and Coaching Psychology. He holds a BCom in Industrial Psychology and Business management, an MBA through the University of the North West, an MA in Coaching Psychology (Work-based Learning) from Middlesex University in the UK as well as a post-graduate certificate in group process consultancy through the University of South Africa.

Dedication

This booklet is dedicated to South Africans or Africans doing business in their respective township or homeland: spaza shops, hawkers, liquor stores, hair salons etc. We are often hard on ourselves not realizing the good work which township enterprisers have carried and carrying on with.

With everyone involved in these project, we thought we bring you this necessary and validated perspective carried in the booklet.

A big thank you to the many who allowed me (Tiisetso) and Spaza News to pick their minds for the direction of the booklet.

You the reader will pick one or more concepts which will work for you in your business world.

About author – Tiisetso Maloma

I am a parallel entrepreneur, African entrepreneurship activist and development economics scholar. I devised the **EBC business model checklist** and authored these 3 books: **Forget The business Plan Use This Short Model**, and **Township Biz Fastrack** and The Anxious Entrepreneur (to be released 2nd half of 2015).

My obsession is with the creativity of finding market penetrating advantages for startups/businesses given their limited resources. Although I can never completely leave behind the anxiety entrepreneurship brings, I do it for recreational purposes. It is about testing.

My interest is active in how one can be economically be creative, i.e. figurative and literally, and create products that appeal to people's need, intrigue and consumption.

Entrepreneurship is a nerve wrecking business when things are not going according to one's wish/plan/luck/desire/need/desperation. My next study or field of play is figuring ways entrepreneurs can attract thought-of and especially unthought-of opportunities i.e. things to do to achieve goals and things to do in between achieving goals. I have found the latter helps take away anxiety and depression.

Here are the present businesses I am publicly involved with: Startup Picnic, Bula Buka and Practice DVD education Games.

I love to do talks and workshops on the topics above. I consult privately to a few individuals and entities. Please visit my blog here www.tiisetsomaloma.com where I archive my thoughts, experiments and experiences.

I ventured and wrestled in various industries including: clothing, music, animation, television. Other past ventures include gabble heights Clothing, Rural Joss Clothing and Bhovas & Sam. Eish, I have failed a lot.

I have published many publications and featured in different broadcast shows: www.Under30CEO.co.za, Kaya FM, SAFM, entrepreneur.co.za, NSBC.org.za, HowWeMadeItInAfrica.com, Business Report; cliffcentral.com, 2000 FM, YFM, Alex FM, Mamelodi FM, Hashtag Radio and many more.

This is as far as my academic education goes: Diploma in Accounting and Post Graduate Diploma in Forensic Auditing, both with the university of Johannesburg.

"Radical with pragmatic economic solutions" Thebe Ikalafeng

"Dresses more like a rock star than an accountant" Deon Maas

Other books by author

Find the books by Tiisetso Maloma on all major online stores such as Amazon, Exlusive Books, iBookstore and Kobo. For print books in South Africa, visit www.tiisetsomaloma.com.

FORGET THE BUSINESS PLAN USE THIS SHORT MODEL

THE ANXIOUS ENTREPRENEUR

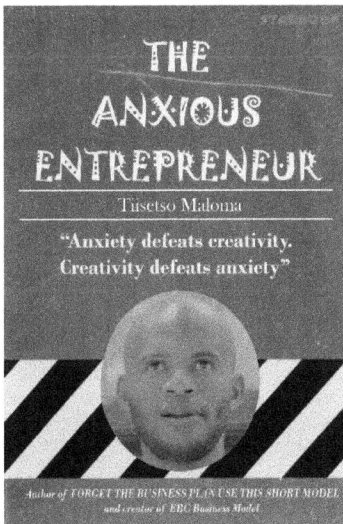

Tools by author: EBC business model checklist

EBC business model checklist

Essential Business Components
by Tiisetso Maloma

1 (ABSOLUTE) PRODUCT

- Serve an identifiable purpose and deliver value to consumer
- Better value from competition, and in the eye of consumer
- Appeal to a need or want
- Deliver efficiency in use
- Easily defined use/s and/or purpose
- Good quality, good after sales service and maintenance
- Well branded for enticement and appeal
- Don't take forever building product
- Protect product use through innovation and consistent enhancement
- Validate use with customers and demographics

3 CASH FLOW

- Make, sell, remake, invest and grow
- Rationalise every cent spent, must be for growth
- Separate business bank account
- As you grow, consolidate expenses for bulk discounts

4 DISTRIBUTION

- How consumers get hold of product
- Or how service is delivered
- *Must be efficient for consumers
- Relate 'absolute product' and 'marketing' to distributor
- Rational is to get customers to store
- Device in-store advertising
- Best absolute service wins

5 RELENTLESS

- Try, fail, you are sharper, you are smarter, retry

2 MARKETING

- Don't target market, mark possible buying targets/groups
- Which group is likely to buy the quickest?
- How to get hold of each group? Which mediums?
- What advertising can I afford? Which medium is free?
- Initial mediums must have highest marked-target concentration
- I cant pay $1000 for ad and make only $500 sales
- Assign a higher priority to which group?
- Which group is inexpensively reachable?
- Sensitivity of group?
- How am I going to penetrate each group?
- Which group will contribute most sales?
- How to relate product to group
- PR - Stories that capture media's attention. Will your story sell their papers? Is it valuable content? Which problems are solved? What are special facts?
- Social media is strong when used to show consumer testimonials
- At least 2 marketing programs for core and conservative markets
- Advertising must have spunk and drama
- Build buzz around product as its in creation, this creates customers in advance

6 HAPPINESS (AND HONESTY)

- Happiness favours a decisive mind
- Indecision obviously is not progress
- Dishonesty is heavy to carry
- Entrepreneurs make plans for progress, not excuses (decisions)
- Always relook at model, it gels, its adds up

EBC business model is detailed in the book, FORGET THE BUSINESS PLAN USE THIS SHORT MODEL, avail @ Amazon and Kobo.co.za. For print copies in SA and business model consultations contact, (m) 072 744 6142, (t) 012 767 8084, (e) info@tiisetsomaloma.com
Visit www.tiisetsomaloma.com

Go here to download a PDF of the business model checklist. EBC stands for Essential business components, its detailed in the book FORGET THE BUSINESS PLAN USE THIS SHORT MODEL.

The EBC business model canvas points out 6 components which are crucial for entrepreneurs to focus on; they fit most business types, and serve as guideline of what is vital in running a profitable, sustaining and growing business.

The EBC model is not limited to venturing by entrepreneurs; it's usable by other value providers such as consultants, freelancers, photographers, musicians, designers, engineers and others.

In one sheet, crucial business essentials are pointed out, to easily remind you.

Introduction

This is a project I hold dear to my heart. As a young boy, 14 years of age, I had worked with my father in running his Spaza shop back home in Schoonoord, Limpopo. In its early days of commencing, it had convenience and/or staple products such as Soft drinks – Sweets – Salt/Sugar, Cigarettes, to name but a few, and later on seeing the business grow and from that strength open doors to other forms of business.

The premise of this booklet it to not scorn township based business. I hold township business owners to high regard. These are the folks that do what most South Africans wish they could do but do not out of fear, and that is: To live their dreams. They get to make money everyday - I envy that. I know most of my entrepreneur friends envy that as well.

In actual fact, township business owners are doing better than most of us.

The most powerful element when it comes to township business is that most of them start from what we call "petty beginnings" - A petty beginning which most dreamers are not willing to undergo. The world has a lot of people wanting to be entrepreneurs, but are held back by the notion that someone has to give them funding. While they wait for funding, others start businesses even from petty beginnings.

Township Biz Fastrack gives insights into development and growth models for township based businesses.

The booklet touches on powerful principles which township business has carried for years, but subconsciously have not applied consistently in the long term. Therefore some haven't grown and sustained themselves amidst heavy competition and ever-changing societal dynamics.

The one principle in the booklet is "bootstrapping," which by example is: Starting off by selling one or two strategic and/or passion products, e.g. atchar, to then reinvesting the proceeds on expansion. Practical learning thus happens with minimum risk in capital investment.

The other principle is "validation." So many businesses which started off selling few items have grown on the strength of customer advice - what to stock further.

The booklet also includes interviews with notable township business owners, whom give strategic survival tactics.

It is targeted at township business owners and employees. It will spark the thinking and conversation on how to grow township business and benefit society to the maximum.

1. WARM UP CHAPTER - Simple and small approaches conquer mountains

A start needs to happen

The Richard Maponya and Herman Mashaba of this world have started from what society would call humble or petty beginnings.

The truth is, wherever you are, you are faced with circumstances. Either limiting or enabling, they are your circumstances regardless.

The other truth is we have ambitions. To achieve our ambitions, we have to swim through our circumstances: Enabling or Limiting.

They approached their ambition. They struggled with finding that door that let them in, but with mistakes, practice and constantly formulating sharper approaches, they finally found that door.

They 'started' within their circumstances: Enabling or Limiting. But I know, no matter how difficult one's circumstances, there is always a first step to take, no matter how small.

The golden principle evident is: For something to be, it must be started. Its not that our township business heroes started from humble or petty beginnings: It is that they started. Your background matters not.

No one wants to start small.
I don't want to start small. But the most liberating thing, I've learned, is starting, no matter how small the step is.

It's not how big the ambition is, but how simpler the approach is made to be.

So many people out there, who want to start businesses but are waiting for the comfortable circumstances. For example, waiting for their kids to grow up, to get fired, to have the best idea and so forth.

I have realized that entrepreneurship is not a way to escape reality. So many people out there believe that once they start a business, challenges and problems will disappear from their lives. I have experienced this as untrue.

It is not as easy as leaving your job, starting a business - then instantly rich.

Entrepreneurship is a way to be part of reality, but as a facilitator or creator of value. It's a part where you are responsible for giving people value or convenience. If you start selling bread in your area, wherein the situation was that people had to walk distances to another area to acquire bread — you have provided value and convenience to them. That is entrepreneurship.

In this way you are being realistic and providing needed or usable solutions.

I'm saying you can start a business while you are employed, its all about providing value which people (your customers) can use to gain convenience or whatever form of value they can use to advance or serve their course - Then build up from there.

It's very smart to start a business while still employed. As long as you are providing usable value and you are honest of your employment. It's a great way to learn with minimum risk.

There are never 100% percent right circumstances to start a business. Just remember starting small is okay, as long as you are providing usable value.

In the next pages, you will discover the advantage and beauty of starting small – then building and growing from what you have learned thus far.

Case study

I was in a consulting session with one lady a while ago. Her passion is to organize children's parties. So, she is looking for funding to buy jumping castles and the likes. She has been doing so for a year now, still no luck.

Recently I have walked through a similar path as her, for an edu-tech startup I'm part of. I miss my own medicine sometimes.

She is serious about this business; otherwise she wouldn't have paid for my services.

Problem

Because her ambitions are big, she believes she needs to start big. Of course she doesn't have the funds to fund her big ambitions. So when her endeavors of getting funding do not go accordingly, it devastates her. A lot of us can relate to this.

Nothing in life is a guarantee. Just because you cannot secure funding for your idea, it doesn't mean there aren't other ways to approach achieving your goal.

Opportunity in solution

She has a beautiful situation, she has a job. She works for a bank as a teller.

How important to her is this dream? Is it just an ideal wish? It all depends on her, on how serious she is about this dream.

What she could do is take out a loan, or save up, to buy one jumping castle while still employed. The advantage in the starting lean approach is it's less of a risk, than if she started with 10 jumping castles and had bought the whole kiddies party equipment. It would be a waste to have 10 jumping castles, which she bought on loan, and are not all bringing in revenue, while still marketing them and paying interest on the loan.

With this one jumping castle, she has the opportunity to validate the market and test few marketing tactics, which then will let her know which equipment to invest into in the future.

First thing: Marketing

The first thing to have after realizing the product/business you would want to sell: Marketing. She needs to know how she will raise awareness on her jumping castle business or the services she renders.

Marketing is how you let possible buyers know of your product. Once you say possible buyers, it means you know they need the product and are willing to buy it.

In her area, there are those who are already offering these services, the question now is: What is it that she is going to add to her services that will set her apart from other businesses so that she is regarded as the preferred supplier? **Secondly**, how will she present (brand) her services?

Finding out if her services are favorable

- Check what others are offering, in her community and other areas?
- Check how others are marketing, in her community and other areas?
- Check her proximity with her competition?
- Which areas are underserved with this service?
- Which equipment is the most sought after, but with enough supply?
- Which equipment is sought after but with rare supply?

Asking herself these questions and investigating them practically, helped her get ideas on how to market her business at first.

The "why" game with customers

A simple resource she has is interviewing the market (possible buyers). She simply has to go around, ask parents their vision of kiddies parties, and insight regarding their good and bad experiences. Explain her vision and see if they would hire her envisioned service. If not, then she can tweak her vision.

The parents will give her problems they have experienced in

dealing with kiddies parties and suppliers. These are gaps she can fill.

This is a simple way of finding out what they are willing to spend on.

The advantage of starting small

- She has an opportunity to **learn without much financial risk**.
- With what she has learned while operating her business with one jumping castle, the **knowledge base will be a great resource in determining how to expand the business and what to invest in**.

2. Bootstrapping

This is a powerful concept which township business has been applying for ages. It is almost the essence of how the township business was born. But it isn't understood fully and that is why it isn't used effectively in the long term.

Bootstrapping is when a business is started with selling few strategic or passion items like atchar, sodas, electricity, etc. I say strategic items because it's mostly items with which they have a niche or whatever advantage over the other. It could be that your beverages are colder, or your atchar has more oil, or none of the nearest shops stock up atchar.

This is the story of most township businesses. They start small with strategic products and invest the proceeds into adding other products gradually. From selling atchar, they could go to selling sodas. *Atchaar goes well with bread, and bread goes well with liquids. Notice the link of these 3 products. They complement each other.*

When a new township business starts off with one product, it will notice other products that the community needs. As it now appreciates the need, it can now stock small amounts of these products to test.

The advantage of starting small is you get to learn with minimum risk.

- -

Every township has a story of an ambitious community member who gets a lump sum - It could be either from a pension fund, lottery winnings, or wherever it could have came from. He then gets ambitious and builds a big business structure, i.e. grocery store, shopping complex, hotel, B&B, etc. I know of some people back at home Ga-Sekhukhune.

Their businesses can either go bad or good. In the case of it going bad, it could be because they ran out of funds prior finishing off their project and seeing it through. Or, the operations of the business do not generate sufficient cash flow to reason up the investment and/or their management is not feasible.

Business is always a noble venture. Yes, the higher the risk the higher the returns possibly. But starting large has the disadvantage in that if you don't have necessary experience, and if you hit a stumbling block, your risk is high as the investment is high.

Even if your research and trend analysis highly favors your venture, it is still risky. Even corporations like Shoprite still run a risk opening a new store, but experience helps them avert the risks.

- -

Humble or Petty beginnings. I do not like this phrase. Let's use the word lean. Starting out smaller or lean, is very smart, it also helps in getting real experience with minimal risk. It gives one an opportunity to expand with feedback from paying customers.

We know of a chisa nyama that started off as a carwash.

There's a chisa nyama in Mamelodi called Motswala's - It was a pub before. It had closed, and it has now reopened. When it reopened, a fence was erected to make up a new and bigger lounge setting.

Since it opened, which has been over a year now, it's been getting additions. Of late I've seen a thatch room lounge being erected.

What is happening in this situation I believe is, the new additional erections are funding themselves and their direction to some extend is powered by customer feedback or suggestions. And I'm sure it will prove profitable, it will be a nicer space for customers.

This is bootstrapping at its best. It's not necessarily a matter of lack of funds which motivates bootstrapping. It's an intelligent tool in that it gives one an opportunity to get expansion feedback from buying customers. This is a situation were customers are saying, "we will buy such a product if you provide it to us."

Bootstrapping steps

- <u>Start with a strategic product(s)</u>: If it's a passion product, you have an advantage in that you are in love with it. Whatever the product, you must have advantage on it, over others.
- <u>Improve on the one product</u>: Selling one or few products gives you an opportunity to learn greatly about business with minimal risk in investment. Feedback from customers will help you improve your

service and product. When sales are not that great, it gives you an opportunity to investigate the "why" and "where" to move to.

- <u>Reinvest proceeds on adding more strategic products based on market feedback and analysis</u>: If maybe your startup product is sodas, I've seen and experienced consumers advising that products like frozen yoghurt, ice cream, and ice blocks be added.

  I was that kid asking spaza shops to stock products which I wished to buy from them, which they didn't keep.

3. Validation

"It's better to measure 10 times and cut once, than to measure once and cut 10 times". I heard this quote in the movie Barbershop. From then it had this tremendous effect on me. It's like that in business.

Spaza shop operators through experience know which bread brand their market/community prefers, they therefore do not order a lot of the less preferred brands. This is validation; this is the consumers telling their local store what they are willing to spend their money on.

Consumers always communicate their consumption preferences, business owners just have to listen and/or ask. Asking and listening are simple but powerful tools of getting information on what the market is willing to spent on.

Validation is exactly what the latter paragraphs of bootstrapping explained – A situation where expansion direction is informed by the consumers.

How to validate

- Interview customers to find out their problems in relation to your line of business or how you can assist or improve.
- Numbers don't lie. Look into your sales reports over and compare different periods. It should tell you buyer patters and preferences over time.

4. Points hindering township business growth and automation

I spent some time researching and interacting with township businesses and its stakeholders writing this booklet. Below are points which considerably in most cases seem to be holding it aback.

NB: Township business is in good shape. It is very important to the country. What needs to be changed or upgraded is the goal posts.

No foresight on business automation.

They get too attached to the business, policing it everyday themselves, therefore they are not able to work on the business but in it. This straps them from growing as businessmen outside the one shop.

It is understood that some businessmen do not want other businesses besides their one shop, especially if the shop is in their house. But the truth is one can't work forever without taking leave. You can try but the body isn't that generous. It needs rest.

Automation means putting processes in place which can be ran by employees, even when you aren't physically present: The business can transact without your presence. By so doing, you are imputing skill and intelligence in your employees. Intelligent and empowered employees mean that they can help you think and analysis trends in the business.

They can help you decipher feedback from customers and plan ahead.

Communicated and written structures mean that your employees can add something to their CV's. This is motivation to them to do their tasks well. You would be here empowering them; they can flourish on with the skill you inculcated in them.

I have encountered cases were spaza shop owners say they are afraid to hire so called 'smart employees 'in fear that they could steal from them. Yes the risk of automation is theft by employees.

But this risk shouldn't be greater than the opportunity to grow a business. In a spaza shop scenario, the owner cannot work in the store, go out to stock or go out to find suitable point-of-sale machines at the same time.

Well growth can fledge to a certain extent even when the owner is employed in the in-store transactions 24/7, but in the long term, they need to multiply themselves to get more things done - An expansion plan which includes personnel is vital.

Having the time to think and relax (recoup) is very important in business.

No understanding on metric of scaling.

In a spaza shop scenario, only a certain number of people within its radius can buy bread there. One can't force bread consumption to double, unless: Nearest competition ceases or the population within the business's radius doubles. With this understanding, a spaza shop can sell only so much of a given product. To grow further they would have to setup other shops elsewhere, or add new products which their competition doesn't have a niche on or add extra value somehow (e.g. lower prices, convenience in delivery).

Added convenience.

In Mamelodi, I normally buy bread on weekends from a shop further away from my house, because it keeps Telkom Mobile airtime, which my closest shops don't keep.

Shops closest to me lose my business just because of airtime. In some cases, I even buy other products from the shops far from home just because of a simple but strategic good such as airtime.

Other factors

Other factors, which Somali traders seem to excel at is: **alternative cheaper products**, good sales service, a good reading of market needs, one stop shopping for electricity, airtime, grocery and others.

5. INTERVIEWS WITH TOWNSHIP BUSINESS OWNERS

In writing the book, I conducted several research methodologies. What is to follow here is interviews which stood out with notable township business owners, the interviews covered very well the principles which I try to convey in this booklet.

Interview with Thulani 'Joozka' Ndlovu

My leader here Thulani Ndlovu, better known in Mamelodi as 'Joozka', runs an internet café called Joozka Technologiez, which he started early 2005, October. Today, it doubles as a tuck-shop.

It's an idea which lingered in his mind for 4 years before he pursued it - He was working as a lab technician at CSIR, and on the side fixing computers for about R800 each. He then realized he was leaving work home to go to work. He then set ways in researching the viability of offering technology solutions to service his Community of Mamelodi.

Finally the passion and gut kicked him enough to resign from his job and start the business. On the 1st of October 2005, he opened doors to his very first business. He used his savings and retirement funds to turn his room into a tech café, offering solutions such as: internet, copying, typing and fixing phones.

Business was slow of course; he distributed nicely designed pamphlets all over Mamelodi, describing his business offerings. It was a passion business; its viability was a little boosted by the confidence which people in his network placed on him by using him to fix their computers.

The marketing only picked up only a month later. As startup business people, we want our businesses to start making sales from day one, without giving a chance for our marketing activities to take effect.

Validation. As the business was bit-by-bit going through traction, the clientele advised that it needed refreshments whilst browsing the net. This led him to stocking soft drinks. N.B as mentioned in the above chapters, customers will give you product ideas on what products will complement their use of your business services. It's simple as people telling you what they are prepared to spend on. You provide such, it's a given sale transaction.

From cold drinks, it led to the community asking him to stock bread, from bread to milk. He admits the Internet business was taking a while to pick up. The tuck-shop led by consumer request, was growing quicker, and was sustaining his business and with that he was able to beef up the Internet café equipment.

He reveals that the Internet business is seasonal; it has sales more during schooling days. During holidays, the tuck-shop helped sustain things.

In business, you have to analyze trends as to where consumer needs are going, for that he often goes to trade shows and does window-shopping.

Employees and training
In any year, he normally employs 2 to 4 people, depending on the needs of the business.

He or his employees conduct training for new employees. The point he emphasizes on employee training is **'customer treatment' and 'product knowledge'**.

Of course delegation is always a challenge but it is essential for a business to grow. Things like theft and employees stealing customers so that they can service them away from the business form part of the troubles he encounters. He concedes that the fear for this shouldn't discourage business owners from hiring and delegating so they can **work on the business instead**

of in the business.

Entrepreneurs with employees should set tactics and controls to monitor their businesses, to lessen the risks that go with delegation and business automation.

Business is an environment where thinking is critical. Asking for advice from other business people is not weakness but strength. One shouldn't think they are the smartest therefore expecting to solve or do everything themselves.

Life in business has humbled me not to think I'm the smartest. In fact, my take is I'm the least smarty. My job is to facilitate in bringing forth value and convenience to the market – even if means recruiting partners to be on my team.

Growth

Thulani is thinking of other ways to grow his tech-solutions business to it just being an Internet café stationed at his house. He realizes the world is changing and if he doesn't change with it or lead it, he will be like other township businesses with old dilapidated buildings.

The growth will be based on devising ways in which he can meet his community's needs, a system if successful, he can duplicate in surrounding townships. I wish this brother luck in his new business phase and the community projects he is involved in.

Interview with Marumo Lekwankwa

My leader here is a kick-ass businessman whom I look up to. He hails from a business inclined family.

After high school,2001, he went on to complete certificates in criminology, victimology and business management (stock keeping and control). He spent some years studying paralegal, which he didn't complete.

As he was heading (Tshwane Leadership Foundation), he was spotted by the organization PEN International to be its assistant manager. Within a short space he went to be logistics manager. He attributes this fate to that with every task he was given, he over performed on it.

In 2008 he decided to go back home to work in the family business in Jane Furse. His family deals mainly in groceries. It is one of the big suppliers in Ga-Sekhukhune competing with the likes of Pick N Pay and Shoprite.

His entry position was doing all the odd jobs necessary, lifting and delivering stuff. He was prepared to start from the bottom and learn all the ropes of the business. Again as in at his previous job, he over performed every task.

This was an era. The era when we had just realized that foreign business owners have entered our townships hard. Many black businesses did crumble and some are crumbling even today.

Marumo's family business wasn't unique to the pressure brought on by Pakistani, Chinese and Somali business owners. He saw an opportunity to promote himself as a businessman, and again to an extent it was serious situation which affected his family's legacy.

So, he started giving advice on how to handle certain transactions. With his advises proving profitable, he had now promoted himself.

Today he is doing very well in businesses, involved in projects away from the family business.

Below are the key points he would love to share with you.

- He realized there was theft and mismanagement of certain areas. He therefore devised controls to measure up to these risks. *If you can't find the solutions yourself, find out how others have overcome, either by asking for advice from other businessmen or professionals, or the Internet.*
- Built personal relationships with suppliers. *In business, it is important that people know you and see your face. Show up. Greet people. Give your appreciation for their service. Make a complaint (I'm not talking of hysteria).*
- Restructured and negotiated better terms: delivery and stocking.
- Strategically started buying in bulk and forced credit.
- Sold strategic item at low prices, accepting low profits on them: Items like washing powder and maize meal. The rational for this was that, if the public saw him as the cheapest on these products, they would assume that he is the cheapest on a lot of products. This discourages his competition from stocking these strategic products, in this fashion they lost out on more customers, as these strategic products are the decider for customers as where to shop.

- He started a saving scheme for stokvels. They would save with him throughout the year and during the Christmas season; they would redeem their savings by buying from him and also getting a guaranteed discount.
- In this fashion, he secured Christmas customers before the season.
- With this security of customers, he was able to buy in bulk before the Christmas season, which is cheaper. Suppliers tend to up their prices during the festive season.
- This was done discreetly so that he couldn't be copied.
- He offered free transport for his customers. He added convenience.
- He started bidding and securing for food parcel contracts from government, with the advantage that he now had low prices than most, on strategic products.
- He only printed catalogues after his supplies, after he has seen their offering, so to be able to beat them on pricing.
- This was the 99 cents era of pricing: R4.99 is an attraction over R5.00. So he went for 85 cent model: R4.85 is much more attractive than R4.99 and R5.
- The foreign business owners started stocking from him from time to time. They still do.
- Black businesses didn't, they wanted to stock were he stocks, given the advantage that he delivered free and had the same prices as his suppliers due to that he bought in bulk to get discounts.
- His observation is, these foreign owners aren't or weren't that cheap, it's just a perception created by the

alternatives they keep and the low prices they set on strategic products.

The tactics above aren't the set rules. There are more I'm sure. The key principle is, to compete or be competitive, always device tactics to have an edge over your competition. Look for new ways to attract customers. Some will fail some will work.

Again I urge that, a truly competitive business is one which always tries to put more value and convenience in the consumer's hands.

6. Foreigner running shops in South African townships

South African township business is busy being dominated (maybe not yet but close) by foreigners from different nations: Somali, Pakistan, India, Asia and various other African countries.

Very often we hear of a community or bandits somewhere in the country having looted and vandalized shops owned by foreign nationals.

Although in some communities foreign business people have integrated well and joined part in the township lifestyles – and procreation - Specifically, various communities in Limpopo – Sekhukhune.

So what are my thoughts on township business being dominated by foreigners at the fall of some native businesses? I totally would favor a situation were local township business is protected by our national government. But it's not an issue to be reversed but at least contained.

The problem is not foreign business owners in townships but our stagnant attitude to change and competing.

In several news reports and articles, linkages have been made of terrorist organizations operating businesses in townships to raise funds for their activities elsewhere in the world. In one article on CNN.com, they label South Africa as having played as ground for "financial and logistical support to facilitation support". Apparently our country is like a fund raising hub for organizations such as Al Shabaab – through township businesses foreigners operate in our townships.

It's known that most foreign business owners in South Africa are organized, maybe because of their religion. It is suspected that they collaborate funds to stock up for the different shops and get bulk buying discounts.

The insinuation or conspiracy of the terrorism linkages is that their foreigner's businesses are funded by international cartels, contrary to the simple brotherly or faith based fund collaborations. Be it as it may, they are kicking ass, and, I mostly struggle find it hard to believe western media.

The real problem

The bigger problem I think for South Africa is that, in business, we don't tend to push the competitive goal post. In no way am I blaming us.

I've scrutinized the price variation between stores owned by foreigners to those by South Africans, there isn't that much significant difference. Lower prices are normally on strategic products like washing powders and sodas. Plus the alternative cheaper beverages offered by the foreigners.

We need to swallow the reality that the world changes, as it changes business also has to change with the changes. Township businessing isn't unique to this phenomenon. The changes are good; a few years ago there weren't many cell phones, few years later they popularized massively, now every second someone needs airtime to stay connected. Therefore there is more business.

These are all opportunities we are forced to embrace. As a businessperson is an opportunity taker, they should be the first to try spot changes in demand patterns and embrace such. Or even try to lead the change in conveniently modeling their businesses to be more competitive.

If we accept the above paragraph, we should take the responsibility to lead.

7.Leveraging and connecting the dots for growth

Growth for shops

Everyone want to make maximum profit, everyone wants their maximum profits to keep growing every year. Again, I will touch on bread: a community cannot double its bread consumption for the sake of maximizing a certain shop's profits. There is a ceiling in the consumption of bread. There is a ceiling in certain products in the context of a stationed shop.

For example, for a spaza shop to maximize sales, given the community and the radius it operates within, it has to:

- Find ways of being competitive (some of the ways are given this booklet) e.g prices, added convenience, added value etc.)
- Add new products which the community needs like electricity, cheap phones etc.
- Rent out space to phone repairers or shoe repairers etc.

But again, even the new products will reach a sale ceiling or climax.

It's the business owner's prerogative to decide where further to move to in business, or what other business to add. Some people are comfortable with one shop without expanding. It is okay, everyone is entitled to their lifestyle.

A point I have to stress is patience. Follow a course until it is satisfactory to you, it wont happen over night.

Hawkers

This is the guy/lady who hawks house-to-house or at the taxi rank - going from taxi to taxi selling sodas or airtime or whatever product of their choice.

This guy uses the following to make his business a success:

He brings **convenience** to customers who are in the taxi waiting upon it to get full. He brings to them convenient items like airtime (the commuters might need to call someone while traveling in the taxi) or sodas (for refreshment and thirst quenching).

Of course his sales margins will vary depending on a number of things like:

- Christmas season has a high passenger volume than other seasons.
- The need of the products he sells. I'm not sure about the need of hair combs at taxi ranks over nail clippers.
- Niche. The airtime market might be fully saturated and the nail clipper guy could make more money than the airtime guys.
- Airtime might move faster than sodas but have low profit margins. He/she has to decide what brings in more money. Competition is still a factor.

There are no set rules; every area has its factors which determine what makes more money. The best tool to inform you on what to sell is, practical experience i.e. testing things out in the market.

Baby steps and patience

Everything happens over time. For some, the above is not big business. As explained in the 1st chapter of the booklet, everyone has their circumstances and has to swim through their circumstances to reach their ambitions, and there is always a step to take however small.

I don't have all the answers and I'm still swimming my way to my dreams. But, patience and baby steps have proved to be a worthy vehicle in getting me closer.

Don't underestimate the value and lessons learned or to be learned in selling one product, then moving on to add others.

Leveraging time

Money is made over time. Some businesses are automated and transact without the owner's daily involvement.

For a hawker, they spend their time bringing convenience to households or commuters in taxis. That is how their time is spent. Their income varies with the households they visit and the households they establish some sort of frequent supply with.

Growing up, there were hawkers whom would supply my grandmother with thatch brooms. They always knew the best time to come check on us: if our brooms haven't worn off. So I'm sure they kept some system of when to visit which households again. In today's times, there are phones; they could simply call to check if their regular customers are not in need of their supplies.

This requires building good relationships.

The best business model for most I'm sure is to reach a point where their business is automated. For hawkers it could include appointing other hawkers. I'm not sure of the feasibility of this, the risk could be that those hawkers could quit and work for themselves. They way to defeat this risk is to offer them something they can't offer themselves: like using the advantage of bulk buying, wherein your prices are cheaper and its not feasible for them to compete with you.

The basic for growing a business is innovating a new way which offers better value from your peers or competition.

Hawking is a good way to make a living, but make sure you save up your funds. As hawking is a great way to raise funds, leverage the savings on something which will ultimately run on automation e.g. a different business, shop or hiring other hawkers. That is if your goal is to grow.

Growth steps
- Offer better and/or exceptional value to stay in the lead in your particular field.

- Multiply yourself. If you are to hire, come up with a better value to offer your employees than if they were to work for themselves.

- Move to another form of business funded by the funds you have raised: A business which allows automation. And in that business, follow what this booklet teaches.

I will give an example with my business model consulting. I can only have so many individual consultations per month, given I'm involved in other businesses. So, I'm trying to leverage this side of the business through talks, workshops, magazine columns, books and others to come. This means I can get paid so much for work which otherwise takes less time than doing a lot of individual consultations.

8. Cry beloved black business, wake up, and move forward into progress

Do not construe this article/chapter as hysterical. Consider the positions offered and take those which you could use to improve your business.

A quick browse in the townships, you will notice a lot of small businesses i.e. spaza-shops, driving schools, internet/printing cafés, pharmacies, etc. Their state of branding hasn't changed in last 7 or more (of course) years.

This is all observation, you welcome to argue, maybe point areas you have observed as improved. There are those areas that went notches up. There are those that lived up to innovation and taken their businesses to future heights.

Another observation is, a lot of business sites (buildings) in rural areas and townships are old and unmaintained. I've observed this in Gauteng, Mpumalanga and Limpopo: Soweto, Jane Furse, Mamelodi, Alexandra, Globlersdal, Witbank, Middelburg.

I'm describing black business. In other instances, this also applies to white owned businesses: Lombardy East, Mayfair (which is Indian) and Silverton.

This is not a for-black-only article. Its basis is on the development to prosperity for South Africa.

Most of these businesses are either ran by old men or young adults (you can say youth). It's probably through inheritance, family responsibility or fresh entrepreneurial venturing.

Given the state of black business in our communities; the lack thereto of progressive maintenance (you have seen old decayed/decaying buildings I'm pointing to) and given the paragraph above. It seems there isn't any form of conscience towards continual maintenance and upgrade. Worryingly, there isn't a sense of best-growth-practice-legacy being left for new entrepreneurs by the old generation businessmen.

It's worrying that most businesses in townships are in decaying shape.

I know some minds are jumping at that I'm bashing black business. Hold those guns playa, I'm not. Reading further will affirm this. It's all in the spirit of building South Africa.

Maponya Mall, now this is an important benchmark in South African democracy. An IT shopping mall, owned by a black man, serving a township community, in South Africa! Of course shopping complexes are always being built in townships, but owned by white businessmen mostly.

The truth about apartheid is that it empowered whites at the disempowerment and oppression of blacks. When democracy was realized in 1994, white business already had leverage over black aspiring enterprisers. Which therefore meant/means Pick N Pay, Shoprite, Edgars etc. were leveraged to move faster in serving black communities fully. So in saying, apartheid was about economics.

We are now post apartheid South Africa, the economic scars of apartheid will take time to vanish, but mostly it depends on us, how fast we swim and innovate. So as black business, its time we pulled our socks up and start respecting money. Let's start putting value forth in attracting business, and use advanced marketing psychologies. It's not helpful to cry blame on apartheid whereas our business development is stagnant.

- - -

Threats to black business, any business, and to South African development (prosperity).

No formulated conscience towards service, store keeping, marketing, and branding.

I've met a lot of small business owners, particularly in black communities, pointing out to problems affecting their business. The number one cry they make is, there isn't business anymore, number 2 is, big business is taking over (white business) and number 3 is the foreigners (Somalis).

Is it that hard for black South African business to overcome and compete, the challenges eluded above?

Baloyi Hair Salon vs. a salon in some mall. A Jet store in Jane Furse vs. a Jet store in Eastgate. I bet you in both cases, the latter stores have better service. Why is it that township (and rural areas) business is not aiming for excellence? Customers are paying in the same currency, which is South African Rands, there isn't anywhere where it says money is better spent at Eastgate. We have to give forth the best value and service for people's monies.

Often it's easy to point to problems and blame everyone but ourselves.

Have the business people I'm talking of ever questioned their service, store keeping, pricing, marketing etc. Have they owned up to the challenges they face (and it doesn't include burning foreigners), that is coming up with solutions to internally and externally improve their businesses.

There isn't a sense of conscience towards sales service. I've worked at a retail shop before, I've worked at a call centre agency, at both of these jobs, training was provided. It's not difficult for black business to keep a standards book, keep maintaining it (improving it) and always relate it to employees. That's how skills would be built and installed.

I'm not alluding to that business service in black communities is horrible, but mostly there isn't a level of conscience towards excellent service.

Enslaving our own people
How much does black business pay its employees? Through a quick assessment, someone who works at Pick N Pay versus someone who works at (made up example) Baloyi Bottle Store, you can tell who earns better, works legal working hours, and is plugged into the banking system.

Whereas it's commendable that our labour unions and government have launched decent working conditions, sadly some (and/or most) black businesses totally derail from these laws.

There are many workers in the townships that work from 7am in the morning, till 11pm, six days a week.

It leads to say, in this fashion, black business isn't contributing to the growth of the greater society, therefore black intellect is deprived growth. As black business we shouldn't only enrich our pockets. Its selfish not to train, pay and treat people decently, it takes away development potential of the country.

When you pay people crappy salaries, they will give crappy service, probably act crappy and affect your business greatly (no good way). All it says is you are a crappy selfish business person. These won't add any value to your business knowledge and development.

No growth conscience
Yet with so many bottles stores, hair salons; we have seen very few

black businesses venture into growth models like franchising, outlets, sister stores.

Yet Tops (Spar) and Pick n Pay Liquor venture into our townships. Some of these franchises are black owned, it is still not enough. We need to sprout out and franchise out stores that we own.

Vital to triumph of black businesses, any business actually.

Let's own up. We are losing business because we do not give our customers reasons to buy from us again. Nothing stays the same. People grow in taste; our businesses should grow as well.

As an entrepreneur, always find solutions to make people buy from your business.

Our business services should be attractive. Therefore there should be service training. This is important even for Spaza-shops, hair salons or bottle stores.

People should know your wonderful store (if it's indeed wonderful), therefore they should be marketing. It's important for shops in townships to be visible. You do not want to miss out on chance buyers.

When one walks into black businesses in townships and rural areas, they should experience: excellent and informed customer service, competitive pricing; and a well cleaned, merchandised and maintained store. We must strive to be the very best.

Tiisetso Maloma

9.Mentors

Business is full of risks. To avert some risks, you need someone with business experience to help you win over some of the risks.

You can have as many mentors as you like to have varying insights. But it is great if one of them has been in the business you are in or you are interested to venture into.

The **advantage of having a mentor is he/she has experience of offering services and value to customers**, he/she knows the best way to give people value.

This is the kind of skill a new entrepreneur needs. **They can direct you to the best suppliers, and even better – introduce you to them.**

I'm thankful to all the senior business people who opened their doors to me when I sought guidance. In most cases, I had nothing to give but just the zeal to learn from them.

Over time I have learned a skill were I add value to them in one way or another. It could be introducing to them to a good graphic designer or supplier or give them online advertising tactics. I ask them their current challenges, if I can help, I try help.

You could be afraid that they would steal your idea, it is fair skepticism. Before asking for a mentor, vet them. When you have identified who can be your mentor, ask around about them, that is how you could find out if they are dubious or not.

As a business person, always verify.

If you are a spaza shop owner and don't want to ask mentorship from a competitor, ask a similar someone in a different area.

Everyone likes to be listened to. Everyone likes to tell their story. One of the best gifts to give a mentor is an ear.